P9-EMG-899

DEVOTIONS
FOR
COMFORT
&HOPE

ISAIAH & 1 PETER

DEVOTIONS
FOR
COMFORT
&HOPE

ISAIAH & 1 PETER

Warren W. Wiersbe

HONOR HB BOOKS

Inspiration and Motivation for the Seasons of Life

COOK COMMUNICATIONS MINISTRIES
Colorado Springs, Colorado • Paris, Ontario
KINGSWAY COMMUNICATIONS LTD
Eastbourne, England

Honor ® is an imprint of
Cook Communications Ministries, Colorado Springs, CO 80918
Cook Communications, Paris, Ontario
Kingsway Communications, Eastbourne, England

DEVOTIONS FOR COMFORT AND HOPE
© 2005 by Warren Wiersbe

Cover Design: Jackson Design CO, LLC/Greg Jackson

First Printing, 2005
Printed in the United States of America

Printing/Year

1 2 3 4 5 6 7 8 9 10   /   10 09 08 07 06 05

This book was originally published as two paperback editions in 1994 and 1995, compiled by Stan Campbell. Each devotional reading is adapted from Warren Wiersbe's "Be" series.

ISBN 1-56292-645-4

Comfort

Thirty Daily Readings from the Book of Isaiah

It is too bad that our English word "comfort" has lost its original meaning of "with strength." The purpose of comfort is not to pamper and protect us, but to strengthen us and enable us to carry the burdens of life and serve the Lord effectively.

God is not a doting grandparent who shelters us from problems and "kisses" our bruises to "make them well." He is a loving Father who wants us to mature and become more like Jesus Christ; and to do that, we must face new challenges and depend on new strength from above.

"O, do not pray for easy lives," said Phillip Brooks. "Pray to be stronger men! Do not pray for tasks equal to your powers. Pray for powers equal to your tasks!" (The Rt. Rev. William Scarlett, DD, Phillip Brooks: *Selected Sermons*, E. P. Dutton & Company, Inc., p. 352). That's what God's comfort is all about: power from God to meet the demands of life and to grow because of them. If we don't grow, we can't tackle bigger tasks and serve God in harder places.

The prophet Isaiah lived in a day similar to our own. The nations were frequently at war; political schemes and alliances changed from day to day; the economy was frequently threatened; the people practiced a routine religion that covered up their hidden idolatry; and few people really wanted to hear the Word of the Lord.

Into this discouraging scene came Isaiah, sharing the comfort—the strength—of the Lord. His major theme was salvation. His major purpose was to give strength to a people who were prone to drift with the current and depend on everything but the Lord.

As you walk with Isaiah, learn to receive God's comfort, and *learn to share it with others*. They need it too.

Shout for joy, O heavens;
rejoice, O earth;
burst into song, O mountains!
For the LORD comforts his people
and will have compassion on his afflicted ones.

ISAIAH 49:13

Day 1

Much Upheaval; Much Comfort

"Comfort, comfort my people, says your God."
ISAIAH 40:1

I saiah is great for two reasons," wrote William Sanford LaSor in his fascinating book *Great Personalities of the Old Testament* (Revell, p. 136): "He lived in momentous days, in critical days of international upheaval, and he wrote what many consider to be the greatest book in the Old Testament." "We see Isaiah move with fearless dignity through the chaos of his day," wrote E. M. Blaiklock, "firm in his quiet faith, sure in his God" (*Handbook of Bible People*, Scripture Union, p. 329).

Isaiah is the prophet we need to hear today as he cries out God's message above the din of world upheaval, "Comfort, comfort my people." The English word "comfort" comes from two Latin words that together mean "with strength." When Isaiah says to us, "Be comforted!" it is not a word of pity, but of power. God's comfort does not weaken us; it strengthens us. God is not indulging us, but empowering us. "In quietness and in confidence shall be your strength" (30:15 KJV).

As we study Isaiah's book, we will meet not only this outstanding prophet, but also some mighty kings and rulers; and we will witness the rise and fall of magnificent kingdoms. We will see God's people chastened and then restored. But above all else, we will see the Lord Jesus Christ, God's "Suffering Servant," as He does the will of God and suffers and dies for the sins of the world.

Applying God's Truth:

1. Can you think back to a time when God's comfort gave you much strength? What did you learn from that experience?

2. What situation(s) are you currently facing where you are in great need of God's comfort?

3. What are your goals (or hopes) as you read through the book of Isaiah?

Day 2

A Prophecy We Can Count On

"The vision concerning Judah and Jerusalem that Isaiah son of Amoz saw."

ISAIAH 1:1

I saiah's name means "salvation of the Lord," and salvation (deliverance) is the key theme of his book. He wrote concerning *five different acts of deliverance* that God would perform: (1) the deliverance of Judah from Assyrian invasion (see chaps. 36–37); (2) the deliverance of the nation from Babylonian captivity (see chap. 40); (3) the future deliverance of the Jews from worldwide dispersion among the Gentiles (see chaps. 11–12); (4) the deliverance of lost sinners from judgment (see chap. 53); and (5) the final deliverance of creation from the bondage of sin when the kingdom is established (see chaps. 60; 66:17).

Sir Winston Churchill was once asked to give the qualifications a person needed in order to succeed in politics, and he replied: "It is the ability to foretell what is going to happen tomorrow, next week, next month, and next year. And to have the ability afterwards to explain why it didn't happen."

Because God's prophets were correct *all of the time,* they didn't have to explain away their mistakes. "If what a prophet proclaims in the name of the LORD does not take place or come true," wrote Moses, "that is a message the LORD has not spoken" (Deut. 18:22). Isaiah wrote: "To the law and to the testimony! If they do not speak according to this word, they have no light of dawn" (Isa. 8:20). Isaiah was a man who had God's light, and he was not afraid to let it shine.

Applying God's Truth:

1. Isaiah's name means "salvation of the Lord." If you were given a name to reflect your spiritual goals or mission, what do you think it might be?

2. In what ways do you think others see God's light shine from your life?

3. What are five "acts of deliverance" that you wish God would perform in your life?

Day 3

Isaiah: A Personality Profile

*"The ox knows his master, the donkey his owner's manger,
but Israel does not know, my people do not understand."*

ISAIAH 1:3

What kind of man was Isaiah the prophet? As you read his prophecy, you will discover that he was *a man in touch with God*. He foresaw God's Son and revealed God's glory, he heard God's message, and he sought to bring the people back to God before it was too late.

Isaiah was *a man who loved his nation*. He was a patriot with a true love for his country, pleading with Judah to return to God and warning kings when their foreign policy was contrary to God's will.

He was also *a man who hated sin and sham religion*. His favorite name for God was "the Holy One of Israel," and he used it twenty-five times in his book. (It was used only five times in the rest of the Old Testament.) He looked at the crowded courts of the temple and cried out, "They have forsaken the LORD; they have spurned the Holy One of Israel and turned their backs on him" (v. 4). Jehovah was holy, but the nation was sinful; and Isaiah called the people to repent.

Isaiah was certainly *a courageous man*. Unafraid to denounce kings and priests, and unwavering when public opinion went against him, he boldly declared the Word of God.

He was *a man skilled in communicating God's truth*. Not content with merely declaring facts, Isaiah clothed those facts in striking language that would catch the attention of a people blind and deaf to spiritual truth. Like our Lord Jesus Christ, Isaiah knew how to stir the imagination of his listeners so that he might arouse their interest and teach them God's truth (see Matt. 13:10–17).

Applying God's Truth:

1. Of all Isaiah's qualities described here, which would you say is most important for a prophet of God? Why?

2. Which of these qualities best describes you?

3. How do you think a person with these characteristics would fit in a nation that has "turned their backs" on God?

Day 4

Religion Gone Wrong

Read Isaiah 1:5–3:26

*"Your hands are full of blood; wash and make yourselves clean.
Take your evil deeds out of my sight! Stop doing wrong, learn to do right!"*

ISAIAH 1:15–17

The disgusting thing about Isaiah's rebellious nation is that they were a *religious people* (see vv. 10–15). They attended temple services and brought a multitude of sacrifices to the Lord; but their hearts were far from God, and their worship was hypocritical. Judah's worship of Jehovah was iniquity, not piety; and God was sick of it!

But before passing judgment on worshipers in a bygone era, perhaps we should confess the sins of the "worshiping church" today. According to researcher George Barna, 93 percent of the households in the United States contain a Bible, and more than 60 percent of the people surveyed claim to be religious; but we would never know it from the way people act. One Protestant church exists for every 550 adults in America, but does all this "religion" make much difference in our sinful society?

The average church allocates about 5 percent of its budget for reaching others with the gospel, but 30 percent for buildings and maintenance. Where churches have life and growth, such construction may be needed; but too often the building becomes "a millstone instead of a milestone," to quote Vance Havner. At least 62 percent of the people Barna surveyed said that the church was not relevant to today's world and was losing its influence on society. (See *The Frog in the Kettle* by George Barna, published by Regal Books.) It may be that, like the worshipers in the ancient Jewish temple, we are only going through the motions.

Applying God's Truth:

1. In what ways are many Christians today "religious," yet with their hearts "far from God"?

2. Would you say you live in "a Christian nation"? Explain.

3. What do you think is the number one problem in the church today?

Day 5

Isaiah's Vision

Read Isaiah 4–6

> *"Then I heard the voice of the Lord saying, 'Whom shall I send?*
> *And who will go for us?' And I said, 'Here am I. Send me!'"*
>
> ISAIAH 6:8

Anyone reading the first few chapters of Isaiah's book might be inclined to ask, "What right does this man have to pronounce judgment on the leaders of the land and the many worshipers in the temple?" The answer is found in chapter 6: Isaiah's account of his call to ministry. Before he announced any "woes" on others, he first confessed his own sin and said, "Woe is me!" He saw the Holy One of Israel, and he could not keep silent.

The sight of a holy God, and the sound of the holy hymn of worship, brought great conviction to Isaiah's heart; and he confessed that he was a sinner. Unclean lips are caused by an unclean heart (see Matt. 12:34–35). Isaiah cried out to be cleansed inwardly, and God met his need. If this scene had been on earth, the coals would have come from the brazen altar where the sacrificial blood had been shed, or perhaps from the censer of the high priest on the Day of Atonement (see Lev. 16:12). Isaiah's cleansing came by blood and fire, and it was verified by the Word of the Lord.

Before we can minister to others, we must permit God to minister to us. Before we pronounce "woe" upon others, we must sincerely say, "Woe is me!" Isaiah's conviction led to confession, and confession led to cleansing (see 1 John 1:9).

"Go and tell" is still God's command to His people. He is waiting for us to reply, "Here am I; send me!"

Applying God's Truth:

1. Do you think today's servants of God are "called" as clearly as Isaiah was? If not, how can they be as sure as Isaiah was that they are doing God's will?

2. Do you feel fully equipped and qualified to "go" wherever God sends you? If not, what would need to be done first?

3. Aside from feeling qualified, are you willing to say, "Here am I. Send me!"? Explain.

Day 6

A Sure Sign

Read Isaiah 7–8

> *"The Lord himself will give you a sign: The virgin will be with child and will give birth to a son, and will call him Immanuel."*
>
> ISAIAH 7:14

These were perilous days for the nation of Judah. Assyria was growing stronger and threatening the smaller nations whose security depended on a very delicate political balance. Syria and Ephraim (the Northern Kingdom) tried to pressure Judah into an alliance against Assyria, but Ahaz, king of Judah, refused to join them. Why? Because he had secretly made a treaty with Assyria! (See 2 Kings 16:5–9.)

If Ahaz had believed God's promise, he would have broken his alliance and called the nation to prayer and praise; but the king continued in his unbelief. Realizing the weakness of the king's faith, Isaiah offered to give a sign to encourage him. But knowing that he was secretly allied with Assyria, how could Ahaz honestly ask the Lord for a special sign? So, instead of speaking only to the king, Isaiah addressed the whole "house of David" and gave the prophecy concerning "Immanuel."

Of course, the *ultimate* fulfillment of this prophecy is in our Lord Jesus Christ, who is "God with us," which is what "Immanuel" means. The virgin birth of Christ is a key doctrine; for if Jesus Christ is not God come in sinless human flesh, then we have no Savior. However, this "sign" had an *immediate* significance to Ahaz and the people of Judah. A woman who was then a virgin would get married, conceive, and bear a son whose name would be "Immanuel." This son would be a reminder that God was with His people and would care for them. It is likely that this virgin was Isaiah's second wife, his first wife having died after his first son was born; and that Isaiah's second son was named both "Immanuel" and "Maher-Shalal-Hash-Baz" (meaning "quick to the plunder, swift to the spoil") (see Isa. 8:1, 3).

Applying God's Truth:

1. Do you identify with any of the weaknesses of King Ahaz? In what ways?

2. What changes might you make in your life if you more fully believed God's promise(s)?

3. What are some clear "signs" that God is active in your life?

Day 7

Come Again

Read Isaiah 9–12

"For to us a child is born, to us a son is given, and the government will be on his shoulders. And he will be called Wonderful Counselor, Mighty God, Everlasting Father, Prince of Peace."

ISAIAH 9:6

The Redeemer will come and bring to the world the dawning of a new day. We know that this prophecy refers to Christ because of the way it is quoted in Matthew 4:15–16. But Isaiah looked beyond the first coming of Christ to His second coming and the establishing of His righteous kingdom.

Isaiah 9:6 declares both the *humanity* ("A child is born") and the *deity* ("A son is given") of the Lord Jesus Christ. The prophet then leaps ahead to the Kingdom Age when Messiah will reign in righteousness and justice from David's throne. God had promised David that his dynasty and throne would be established forever, and this promise is fulfilled literally in Jesus Christ who will one day reign from Jerusalem.

If His name is "Wonderful," then there is nothing dull about His reign! As "Counselor," He has the wisdom to rule justly, and as the "Mighty God," He has the power to execute His wise plans. "Everlasting Father" does not suggest that the Son is also the Father, for each person in the Godhead is distinct. "Father of Eternity" is a better translation. Among the Jews, the word "father" means "originator" or "source." For example, Satan is the "father [originator] of lies"

(John 8:44). If we want anything eternal, we must get it from Jesus Christ; He is the "Father of Eternity."

Applying God's Truth:

1. Isaiah saw not only the *coming* of Christ, but His *second coming* as well. How might your spiritual life change if you focused more on the future?

2. What do you most appreciate about the *humanity* of Jesus? What do you most appreciate about His *deity?*

3. Of the titles given the Messiah, which gives you most encouragement? Why?

Day 8
The Mighty Keep Falling

Read Isaiah 13–18

"How you have fallen from heaven, O morning star, son of the dawn! You have been cast down to the earth, you who once laid low the nations!"

ISAIAH 14:12

I saiah warned that the kingdom of Judah would be taken into captivity by Babylon, and this happened in 586 BC. Jeremiah prophesied that the captivity would last for seventy years. Then Babylon would be judged and the Jews permitted to go home. So, the capture of Babylon by Darius the Mede would be good news to the Jews; for it would mean the end of their exile and bondage.

The picture in Isaiah 14:1–23 is that of a mighty monarch whose pride brought him to destruction. This is what happened to Belshazzar when Darius captured Babylon in 539 BC Isaiah described the king's arrival in *sheol,* the world of the dead, where the king's wealth, glory, and power vanished. The dead kings already in sheol stood in tribute to him (see v. 9), but it was all a mockery. Death is the great leveler; there are no kings in the world of the dead. Lucifer (see v. 12 KJV) is Latin for "morning star" and suggests that this king's glory did not last very long. The morning star shines but is soon swallowed up by the light of the sun.

The name Lucifer also indicates that Satan tries to imitate Jesus Christ, who is "the bright and morning star" (Rev. 22:16 KJV). "I will be like the most High" (Isa. 14:14 KJV) reveals his basic strategy, for he is an imitator. Like the king of Babylon, Satan will one day be humiliated and defeated. He will be cast out of heaven and finally cast into hell. Whether God is dealing with kings or angels, Proverbs 16:18 is still true: "Pride goes before destruction, a haughty spirit before a fall."

Applying God's Truth:

1. What was the difference between the "fall" of Judah (God's people) and the "falls" of the surrounding Gentile nations?

2. In what ways do some people today sinfully strive to "be like the most High"?

3. What is the difference between Lucifer's desire to "be like the most High" and a Christian's attempt to be more "Christlike"?

Day 9

International News

Read Isaiah 19–23

> *"In that day Israel will be the third, along with*
> *Egypt and Assyria, a blessing on the earth."*
>
> ISAIAH 19:24

Chapters 13 through 23 of Isaiah teach us some important lessons. First, *God is in control of the nations of the world, and He can do with them what He pleases.* "Though the mills of God grind slowly, yet they grind exceeding small" (Friedrich von Logau, translated by Henry Wadsworth Longfellow). Second, *God especially hates the sin of pride* (see Isa. 13:11; 16:6; 23:9; and Prov. 8:13). When nations turn from the living God to trust their wealth and their armaments, God must show them that He is the only sure refuge. Third, *God judges the nations for the way they treat each other.* Judah was the only nation mentioned that had God's law, yet God held the other ten Gentile nations accountable for what they did. Finally, *God always gives a word of promise and hope to His people.* Babylon will fall, but God will care for Judah (see Isa. 14:1–3, 32). Moab will not accept sanctuary from Jerusalem, but God will one day establish Messiah's throne there (see 16:5). Assyria and Egypt may be avowed enemies of Judah, but one day the three nations will together glorify God (see 19:23–25).

Therefore, no matter how frightening the national or international situation may become, God's children can have peace because they know that Almighty God is on His throne. The nations may rage and plot against God, but "the One enthroned in heaven laughs" (Ps. 2:4). When the Lord of heaven and earth is our Father, and we gladly wear Christ's yoke, we have nothing to fear.

Applying God's Truth:

1. When you consider the turmoil around the world, what are some of your biggest fears?

2. What difference does it make in your personal life to believe that "God is in control of the nations of the world"?

3. In spite of national and international problems, what would you say is God's "word of promise and hope" to His people today?

Day 10
Seeking Refuge

Read Isaiah 24–25

"You have been a refuge for the poor, a refuge for the needy in his distress,
a shelter from the storm and a shade from the heat."

Isaiah 25:4

Isaiah paints two pictures: the buffeting of a storm and the beating down of a burning sun in the desert. Where can travelers go for refuge? They see a huge rock and find refuge in it. God is that rock, and He will be a refuge for His believing people during that terrible day of the Lord. The victory shouts of the enemy will disappear the way heat vanishes when a cloud covers the sea.

God cares for His own in times of trial and judgment. He kept Noah and his family alive through the Flood and guarded Israel when His judgments fell on Egypt. He protected believing Rahab and her family when Jericho fell and preserved a faithful remnant when Judah was taken into Babylonian captivity. Throughout the centuries, He has kept His church in spite of the attacks of Satan and will deliver His church from the wrath to come. When the day of the Lord comes to this godless world, God will see to it that the Jewish remnant will be preserved. "Hide yourselves for a little while until his wrath has passed by. See, the LORD is coming out of his dwelling to punish the people of the earth for their sins" (26:20–21).

Applying God's Truth:

1. What are some of the current "storms" in your life—the emotionally upsetting situations you face?

2. What are your current sources of "heat"—stress, pressure, and so forth?

3. In what ways is God a refuge for each of the situations you have listed? How can you more fully experience His loving protection?

Day 11

The Grapes of Resistance

Read Isaiah 26–27

*"Sing about a fruitful vineyard: I, the LORD, watch over it; I water it continually.
I guard it day and night so that no one may harm it. I am not angry."*

ISAIAH 27:2–4

Isaiah saw both the Israel of his day and the Israel of the future day when God's kingdom would be established. God was not angry with His people; He just yearned for them to return to Him and fervently trust Him. He used war (Assyria) to punish the Northern Kingdom, and captivity (Babylon) to discipline the Southern Kingdom, but He did so in love and not in anger.

In the day of the Lord, God will use suffering to purge His people and prepare them for their kingdom. Isaiah 27:9 does not suggest that personal suffering can atone for sin, for only the sacrifice of Jesus Christ can do that. God uses suffering as a discipline to bring us to submission so that we will seek Him and His holiness (see Heb. 12:1–11). The Babylonian captivity cured the Jews of their idolatry once and for all.

In Isaiah's day, the vineyard was producing wild grapes, but in the future kingdom, Israel will be fruitful and flourishing. God will guard His people and give them all that they need to bring glory to His name. The nation will "bud and blossom and fill all the world with fruit" (Isa. 27:6).

The Bible speaks of three vines: the people of Israel (see v. 5), Christ and His church (see John 15:1–17), and godless Gentile society, "the vine of the earth" (see Rev. 14:18 KJV). The vineyard of Israel was not bearing fruit, the "vine of the earth" was filling the world with poisonous fruit, and God's people had to be faithful branches in the Vine and produce fruit that glorified God's name.

Applying God's Truth:

1. How would you describe your current spiritual life in terms of a vineyard?

2. What are some evidences of "fruit" due to God's involvement in your life?

3. Looking back, can you see how God has worked to make you more productive for Him? Can you cite specific instances?

Day 12

Misusing a Good Gift

Read Isaiah 28

"Priests and prophets stagger from beer and are befuddled with wine;
they reel from beer, they stagger when seeing visions,
they stumble when rendering decisions."

ISAIAH 28:7

Like all devout Jews, Isaiah loved Jerusalem, the holy city, the city of David, the place of God's dwelling. But Isaiah saw storm clouds gathering over the city and announced that trouble was coming. He began his message announcing God's judgment on Ephraim (see vv. 1–6). Their arrogance was detestable to God, for they thought their fortress city of Samaria was impregnable. Samaria reigned in luxury and pleasure and had no fear of her enemies.

The Lord was also appalled by their drunkenness. To the Jews, wine was a gift from God and a source of joy. The law did not demand total abstinence, but it did warn against drunkenness.

A government official in Washington, D.C., once quipped, "We have three parties in this city: the Democratic Party, the Republican Party, and the cocktail party." Indeed, Washington, D.C., ranks high on the list of cities noted for alcohol consumption. Many people don't realize that alcohol and nicotine, America's favorite legal drugs, do far more damage than all the illegal drugs combined. According to Dr. Arnold Washton and Donna Boundy, MSW, alcohol and nicotine kill 450,000 people annually, while illegal drugs kill about 6,000 (*Willpower's Not Enough*, Harper & Row, 1989, p. 13). What hope is there for our affluent, pleasure-loving society that gives lip service to religion and ignores the tragic consequences of sin and the judgment that is sure to come?

Applying God's Truth:

1. What would you say if a non-Christian friend asked, "What does the Bible say about drinking?"

2. Drunkenness was related to arrogance for the people of Ephraim. Do you think the two traits are still related? In what ways?

3. What advice and/or warning would you give a young person just beginning to start drinking on a regular basis? What would you tell an adult who seems to be addicted?

Day 13

Awaiting God's Balance

Read Isaiah 29

"Once more the humble will rejoice in the LORD; the needy will rejoice in the Holy One of Israel. The ruthless will vanish, the mockers will disappear."

ISAIAH 29:19–20

I saiah asked the people to look ahead and consider what God had planned for them. In their political strategy, they had turned things upside down, but God would one day turn everything around by establishing His glorious kingdom on earth. The devastated land would become a paradise, the disabled would be healed, and the outcasts would be enriched and rejoice in the Lord. There would be no more scoffers or ruthless people practicing injustice in the courts. The founders of the nation, Abraham and Jacob, would see their many descendants all glorifying the Lord.

In light of this glorious future, why should Judah turn to feeble nations like Egypt for help? God was on their side, and they could trust Him! God cared for Jacob during all of his years of trial, and surely He could care for Jacob's children. It is tragic when a nation forgets its great spiritual heritage and turns from trusting the Lord to trusting the plans and promises of people.

At the Constitutional Convention in Philadelphia in 1787, Benjamin Franklin said, "I have lived, Sir, a long time, and the longer I live, the more convincing the proofs I see of this truth—*that God governs in the affairs of men.* I therefore beg leave to move that

henceforth prayers imploring the assistance of heaven and its blessings on our deliberations be held in this Assembly every morning."

Isaiah sought that attitude in Jerusalem, but instead, he found
only scoffing and unbelief.

Applying God's Truth:

1. Have you ever gotten yourself in trouble by making a bad
alliance with a person or group rather than seeking God's help? What
were the circumstances and consequences?

2. Are you currently in any cumbersome situations that you would
like to be free of? What do you think God would have you do?

3. How can you ensure that your future decisions will reflect
God's will for your life rather than someone else's?

Day 14

Whom Do You Trust?

Read Isaiah 30–31

> *"Assyria will fall by a sword that is not of man;*
> *a sword, not of mortals, will devour them."*
>
> ISAIAH 31:8

Judah's faith was in people, not in God. They trusted in the legs of horses and the wheels of chariots, not in the hand of the Lord. Why should the Lord fear the Assyrians? Does a lion fear a flock of sheep and their shepherds? Do the eagles fear as they hover over their young in the nest? God would pounce on Assyria like a lion and swoop down like an eagle, and that would be the end! In one night, the Assyrian army was wiped out (see 37:36).

Think of the money Judah would have saved and the distress they would have avoided had they only rested in the Lord their God and obeyed His will. All their political negotiations were futile and their treaties worthless. They could trust the words of the Egyptians but not the Word of God!

As God's church today faces enemies and challenges, it is always a temptation to turn to the world or the flesh for help. But our first response must be to examine our hearts to see if there is something we need to confess and make right. Then we must turn to the Lord in faith and obedience and surrender to His will alone. We must trust Him to protect us and fight for us.

A friend of mine kept a card on his office desk that read: "Faith Is Living Without Scheming." In one statement, that is what Isaiah was saying to Judah and Jerusalem; and that is what he is saying to us today.

Applying God's Truth:

1. Do you agree that "Faith Is Living Without Scheming"? What, exactly, do you think that means?

2. What can you do to remain patient and faithful while waiting for God to act on your behalf?

3. What are some sources of help that even good people tend to turn to rather than trusting God?

Day 15

A Hopeful Forecast

Read Isaiah 32–33

> *"The LORD is our judge, the LORD is our lawgiver,*
> *the LORD is our king; it is he who will save us."*
>
> ISAIAH 33:22

In 1919, American writer Lincoln Steffens visited the Soviet Union to see what the Communist revolution was accomplishing; and in a letter to a friend, he wrote, "I have seen the future, and it works." If he were alive today, he would probably be less optimistic; but in those days, "the Russian experiment" seemed to be dramatically successful.

A university professor posted a sign on his study wall that read, "The future is not what it used to be." Since the advent of atomic energy, many people wonder if there is any future at all. Albert Einstein said that he never thought about the future because it came soon enough!

In Isaiah 32–35, the prophet invites us to look at future events to see what God has planned for His people and His world. In Isaiah 32:1, he writes about *"a* king"; but in 33:17, he calls him *"the* king." By the time we get to verse 22, He is *"our* king." It is not enough to say that Jesus Christ is "a king" or even "the King." We must confess our faith in Him and say with assurance that He is "our King."

In contrast to the evil rulers of Isaiah's day, Messiah will reign in *righteousness* and *justice*. In addition, the King will be like a rock of refuge for the people and like a refreshing river in the desert (see 32:2–3).

Isaiah ministered to spiritually blind, deaf, and ignorant people; but in the kingdom, all will see and hear God's truth as well as understand and obey it. This will happen because the nation will have a new heart and enter into a New Covenant with the Lord (see Ezek. 36:26; Jer. 31:31).

Applying God's Truth:

1. What people do you know who would agree that Jesus is *a* king? *The* King? *Our* King?

2. Right this minute, what are some of your worries about the future? If you *really* trust God, why do you think you are still worried?

3. In what ways has God been like "a refreshing river in the desert" for you in the past? What does that suggest about your future?

Day 16

The Road Less Traveled

Read Isaiah 34–35

"A highway will be there; it will be called the Way of Holiness. The unclean will not journey on it; it will be for those who walk in that Way."

ISAIAH 35:8

I saiah 35:8 expresses one of Isaiah's favorite themes: the highway (see 11:16; 19:23; 40:3; 62:10). During the Assyrian invasion, the highways were not safe (see 33:8), but during the Kingdom Age it will be safe to travel. There will be one special highway: "the Way of Holiness." In ancient cities, there were often special roads that only kings and priests could use; but when Messiah reigns, *all of His people* will be invited to use this highway. Isaiah pictures God's redeemed, ransomed, and rejoicing Jewish families going up to the yearly feasts in Jerusalem to praise their Lord.

When Isaiah spoke and wrote these words, it is likely that the Assyrians had ravaged the land, destroyed the crops, and made the highways unsafe for travel. The people were cooped up in Jerusalem, wondering what would happen next. The remnant was trusting God's promises and praying for God's help, and God answered their prayers. If God kept His promises to His people centuries ago and delivered them, will He not keep His promises in the future and establish His glorious kingdom for His chosen people? Of course He will!

The future is our friend when Jesus Christ is our Savior.

Applying God's Truth:

1. In what way is your spiritual journey like going down a highway?

2. Do you feel completely safe as you travel "the Way of Holiness"? If not, how could you feel safer?

3. How can you be sure you stay on the right highway without taking any wrong turns?

Day 17

A King to Relate To

Read Isaiah 36

"In the fourteenth year of King Hezekiah's reign, Sennacherib king of Assyria attacked all the fortified cities of Judah and captured them."

ISAIAH 36:1

Except for David and Solomon, no king of Judah is given more attention or commendation in Scripture than Hezekiah. "Hezekiah trusted in the LORD, the God of Israel. There was no one like him among all the kings of Judah, either before him or after him" (2 Kings 18:5).

He began his reign about 715 BC, though he may have been co-regent with his father as early as 729 BC. He restored the temple facilities and services of worship, destroyed the idols and the hill shrines where the people falsely worshiped Jehovah, and sought to bring the people back to vital faith in the Lord. He led the people in a nationwide two-week celebration of Passover and invited Jews from the Northern Kingdom to participate.

After the fall of the Northern Kingdom in 722 BC, Judah had constant problems with Assyria. Hezekiah finally rebelled against Assyria (see v. 7); and when Sennacherib, the Assyrian king, threatened to attack, Hezekiah tried to bribe him with tribute (see vv. 13–16). It was a lapse of faith on Hezekiah's part that God could not bless. Sennacherib accepted the treasures but broke the treaty (see Isa. 33:1) and invaded Judah in 701 BC. The account of God's miraculous deliverance of His people is found in Isaiah 36–37.

Chapters 36–39 teach us some valuable lessons about faith, prayer, and the dangers of pride. Though the setting today may be different, the problems and temptations are still the same; for Hezekiah's history is our history, and Hezekiah's God is our God.

Applying God's Truth:

1. Prior to this reading, how much did you know about King Hezekiah? (For further research, see 2 Kings 18–20; 2 Chron. 29–32; and Isa. 36–39.)

2. When you, like Hezekiah, "inherit" something that all your predecessors have made a mess of, do you tend to do what's easy and go with the flow, or do what's hard and correct the situation? What are some examples?

3. What do you think made Hezekiah so different from the kings who preceded him? What can you learn from his example?

Day 18

No Problem Too Big

Read Isaiah 37

> *"The angel of the LORD went out and put to death a hundred and eighty-five thousand men in the Assyrian camp.... So Sennacherib king of Assyria broke camp and withdrew."*
>
> ISAIAH 37:36–37

Sennacherib boasted of his military might and his great conquests, for no obstacle stood in his way. If he so desired, like a god, he could even dry up the rivers! (See v. 25.) But the king of Assyria forgot that he was only God's tool for accomplishing His purposes on the earth, and the tool must not boast against the Maker (see 10:5–19). God would humble Sennacherib and his army by treating them like cattle and horses, leading them away from Jerusalem (see 37:7, 29).

The Assyrian commander had joked that one Assyrian junior officer was stronger than 2,000 Jewish horsemen (see 36:8–9), but it took only one of God's angels to destroy 185,000 Assyrian soldiers! Isaiah had prophesied the destruction of the Assyrian army. God would mow them down like a forest (see 10:33–34), devastate them with a storm (see 30:27–30), and throw them into the fire like garbage on the city dump (see vv. 31–33).

But that was not all. After Sennacherib left Judah, a defeated man, he returned to his capital city of Nineveh. Twenty years later, as a result of a power struggle among his sons, Sennacherib was assassinated by two of his sons in fulfillment of Isaiah's prophecy (see 37:7); and it happened in the temple of his god! (See v. 38.) The field commander had ridiculed the gods of the nations, but Sennacherib's own god could not protect him.

Applying God's Truth:

1. Do you know bullies like Sennacherib? How do you handle such abusive people?

2. How do you feel when you seem tremendously outnumbered? Why?

3. What can you learn from this story to apply to stressful situations you are currently facing?

Day 19

Miracle Recovery

Read Isaiah 38–39

"In those days Hezekiah became ill and was at the point of death. The prophet Isaiah son of Amoz went to him and said, 'This is what the LORD says: Put your house in order, because you are going to die; you will not recover.'"

ISAIAH 38:1

H ezekiah was an author of psalms (see 38:20) and supervised a group of scholars who copied the Old Testament Scriptures (see Prov. 25:1). In the beautiful meditation in Isaiah 38, the king tells us how he felt during his experience of illness and recovery. He had some new experiences that made him a better person.

For one thing, God gave him *a new appreciation of life* (see vv. 9–12). We take life for granted until it is about to be taken from us, and then we cling to it as long as we can. Hezekiah pictured death as the end of a journey, a tent taken down, and a weaving cut from the loom. Life was hanging by a thread!

He also had *a new appreciation of prayer* (see vv. 13–14). Were it not for prayer, Hezekiah could not have made it. At night, the king felt like a frail animal being attacked by a fierce lion; and in the daytime, he felt like a helpless bird. During this time of suffering, Hezekiah examined his own heart and confessed his sins, and God forgave him.

The king ended with *a new appreciation of opportunities for service* (see vv. 15–20). There was a new humility in his walk, a deeper love for the Lord in his heart, and a new song of praise on his lips. He had a new determination to praise God all the days of his life, for now those days were very important to him.

Applying God's Truth:

1. Since Isaiah was God's prophet, and God's prophets were always correct, why do you think Hezekiah prayed for more time after God had said he would not recover?

2. Do you think this is a case where God actually changed His mind? Explain.

3. What can you remember from this story the next time you are facing a seemingly hopeless and final situation?

Day 20

Reading the IBV (Isaiah Bible Version)

Read Isaiah 40:1–26

*"Comfort, comfort my people, says your God.... The grass withers
and the flowers fall, but the word of our God stands forever."*

ISAIAH 40:1, 8

The book of Isaiah can be called "a Bible in miniature." There are
sixty-six chapters in Isaiah and sixty-six books in the Bible. The
thirty-nine chapters in the first part of Isaiah may be compared to the
Old Testament with its thirty-nine books, and both focus primarily on
God's judgment of sin. The twenty-seven chapters of the second part
may be seen to parallel the twenty-seven books of the New
Testament, and both emphasize the grace of God.

The "New Testament" section of Isaiah opens with the ministry of
John the Baptist (see 40:3–5; Mark 1:1–4) and closes with the new
heavens and the new earth (see Isa. 65:17; 66:22). At the heart of the
"New Testament" section of Isaiah's book is our Lord Jesus Christ and
His sacrifice on the cross for our sins (see 52:13–15; 53:1–12). No
wonder Isaiah has been called "the evangelical prophet."

As you study Isaiah 40–66, keep in mind that it was originally
addressed to a group of discouraged Jewish refugees who faced a
long journey home and a difficult task when they got there. Note
how often God says to them, "Fear not!" and how frequently He
assures them of His pardon and His presence. It is no surprise that
God's people for centuries have turned to these chapters to find

assurance and encouragement in the difficult days of life; for in these messages, God says to all of His people, "Be comforted!"

Applying God's Truth:

1. Isaiah's message was that something better was coming in the future. Do God's people still need that message? Why?

2. In what ways do you relate with people who are discouraged and have difficult tasks?

3. How many circumstances can you think of where you long to hear God say, "Fear not! Be comforted"?

Day 21

Plod While You Wait

Read Isaiah 40:27–44:28

"Those who hope in the LORD will renew their strength. They will soar on wings like eagles; they will run and not grow weary, they will walk and not be faint."

ISAIAH 40:31

God knows how we feel and what we fear, and He is adequate to meet our every need. We can never obey God in our own strength, but we can always trust Him to provide the strength we need (see Phil. 4:13). If we trust ourselves, we will faint and fall; but if we wait on the Lord by faith, we will receive strength for the journey. The word "wait" in the King James Version of Isaiah 40:31 does not suggest that we sit around and do nothing. It means "to hope," to look to God for all that we need. This involves meditating on His character and His promises, praying, and seeking to glorify Him.

The word "renew" means "to exchange," as taking off old clothes and putting on new. We exchange our weakness for His power (see 2 Cor. 12:1–10). As we wait before Him, God enables us to soar when there is a crisis, to run when the challenges are many, and to walk faithfully in the day-by-day demands of life. *It is much harder to walk in the ordinary pressures of life than to fly like the eagle in a time of crisis.*

"I can plod," said William Carey, the father of modern missions. "That is my only genius. I can persevere in any definite pursuit. To this I owe everything."

The greatest heroes of faith are not always those who seem to be soaring; often they are the ones who are patiently plodding. As we wait on the Lord, He enables us not only to fly higher and run faster, but also to *walk longer*. Blessed are the plodders, for they eventually arrive at their destination!

Applying God's Truth:

1. What do you find most difficult about waiting upon and hoping in the Lord? Why?

2. When are some times you have flown like an eagle during a crisis?

3. What are three things you can do to be sure you keep plodding ahead every day?

Day 22

Get Out of Babylon!

Read Isaiah 45–48

> *"See, I have refined you, though not as silver;*
> *I have tested you in the furnace of affliction."*
>
> ISAIAH 48:10

The Jews had become comfortable and complacent in their Babylonian captivity and did not want to leave. They had followed the counsel of Jeremiah (see Jer. 29:4–7) and had built houses, planted gardens, and raised families; and it would not be easy for them to pack up and go back to the Holy Land. *But that was where they belonged and where God had a work for them to do.* God told them that they were hypocritical in using His name and identifying with His city but not obeying His will (see Isa. 48:1–2). They were stubborn and were not excited about the new things God was doing for them.

Had they obeyed the Lord in the first place, they would have experienced peace and not war (see vv. 18–19), but it was not too late. He had put them into the furnace to refine them and prepare them for their future work. "Leave Babylon" (v. 20) was God's command. God promised that He would go before them and prepare the way, and they had nothing to fear.

One would think that the Jews would have been eager to leave their "prison" and return to their land to see God do new and great things for them. They had grown accustomed to the security of bondage and had forgotten the challenges of freedom. The church today can easily grow complacent with its comfort and affluence. God may have to put us into the furnace to remind us that we are here to be *servants* and not *consumers* or *spectators*.

Applying God's Truth:

1. How do Christians today become complacent with the "captivity" of sin?

2. When were some times you could have avoided a lot of trouble if you had obeyed God "in the first place"?

3. How is your character refined in the "furnace of affliction"?

Day 23

Gentile Light

Read Isaiah 49

*"I will also make you a light for the Gentiles, that you
may bring my salvation to the ends of the earth."*

ISAIAH 49:6

Messiah came as both a servant and a warrior, serving those who
trust Him and ultimately judging those who resist Him. All of
God's servants should be like prepared weapons. "It is not great tal-
ents God blesses so much as great likeness to Jesus," wrote Robert
Murray McCheyne. "A holy minister [servant] is an awful weapon in
the hand of God."

The Jewish nation was called to glorify God and be a light to
the Gentiles, but they failed in their mission. This is why the
Servant is called "Israel" in verse 3: He did the work that Israel was
supposed to do. Today, the church is God's light in this dark world,
and like Israel, we seem to be failing in our mission to take the
good news to the ends of the earth. We cannot do the job very
effectively when only 5 percent of the average local church budget
is devoted to evangelism!

As Jesus Christ ministered on earth, especially to His own people
Israel, there were times when His work seemed in vain (see v. 4). The
religious leaders opposed Him, the disciples did not always understand Him, and those He helped did not always thank Him. He lived
and labored by faith, and God gave Him success.

Our Lord could not minister to the Gentiles until first He ministered to the Jews (see vv. 5–6). He was despised by both Jews and Gentiles, but He did God's work and was glorified.

Applying God's Truth:

1. Can you think of any groups of people whom you tend to over-look as potential recipients of the gospel?

2. In what ways might the "light" of the church shine brighter in today's world?

3. How could your own "light" brighten a little more gloom than usual today?

Day 24

Complete Submission

Read Isaiah 50–51

> *"Because the Sovereign LORD helps me, I will not be disgraced. Therefore*
> *have I set my face like flint, and I know I will not be put to shame."*
>
> ISAIAH 50:7

The emphasis in this portion of Isaiah is on the Servant's submission to the Lord God in every area of His life and service. His *mind* was submitted to the Lord God so that He could learn His Word and His will (see v. 4). Everything Jesus said and did was taught to Him by His Father. He prayed to the Father for guidance and meditated on the Word. What God taught the Servant, the Servant shared with those who needed encouragement and help. The Servant set a good example for all who know the importance of a daily "quiet time" with the Lord.

The Servant's *will* was also yielded to the Lord God. A "wakened ear" (v. 4) is one that hears and obeys the voice of the Master. The people to whom He ministered were neither "willing" nor "obedient" (1:19), but the Servant did gladly the will of the Lord God. This was not easy, for it meant yielding His body to wicked men who mocked Him, whipped Him, spat on Him, and then nailed Him to a cross.

The Servant did all of this by *faith* in the Lord God. He was determined to do God's will even if it meant going to a cross, for He knew that the Lord God would help Him. The Servant was falsely accused, but He knew that God would vindicate Him and eventually put His enemies to shame. Keep in mind that when Jesus Christ was ministering here on earth, He had to live by faith even as we must today. He did not use His divine powers selfishly for Himself but trusted God and depended on the power of the Spirit (see Phil. 2:5–11).

Applying God's Truth:

1. Do you need to more fully submit your mind to God? Your will? Your body? How can you make any needed changes?

2. What connections do you detect between faith and submission?

3. How does feeling disgrace or shame affect your spiritual growth? How can you deal with any problems in these areas?

Day 25

Sounds of Silence

Read Isaiah 52

"So will he sprinkle many nations, and kings
will shut their mouths because of him."

Isaiah 52:15

The people whose mouths dropped open with astonishment at the Servant's humiliation and exaltation will shut their mouths in guilt when they hear His proclamation. Paul interprets this proclamation as the preaching of the gospel to the Gentile nations (see Rom. 15:20–21). "So that every mouth may be silenced and the whole world held accountable to God" (3:19).

Many people have been tortured and killed in an inhumane way, but knowing about their suffering does not touch our conscience, though it might arouse our sympathy. Our Lord's sufferings and death were different, because *they involved everybody in the world.* The gospel message is not "Christ died," for that is only a fact in history, like "Napoleon died." The gospel message is that "Christ died *for our sins*" (see 1 Cor. 15:3). You and I are as guilty of Christ's death as Annas, Caiaphas, Herod Antipas, and Pilate.

Now we see why people are astonished when they understand the message of the gospel: This man whom they condemned has declared that they are condemned unless they turn from sin and trust Him. *We cannot rejoice in the good news of salvation until first we face the bad news of condemnation.* Jesus did not suffer and die because He was guilty, but because we were guilty. People are astonished at this fact; it shuts their mouths.

Applying God's Truth:

1. Can you recall a time when you received news that left you completely speechless?

2. What are some problems that you know about, yet that haven't really touched your conscience?

3. How do you feel when you dwell on the fact that Christ died for your sins?

Day 26

Sinless and Silent

Read Isaiah 53

> *"He was oppressed and afflicted, yet he did not open his mouth;*
> *he was led like a lamb to the slaughter, and as a sheep before her*
> *shearers is silent, so he did not open his mouth."*

ISAIAH 53:7

Isaiah 53:7 speaks of Jesus' silence under suffering and verse 8 of His silence when illegally tried and condemned to death. In today's courts, a person can be found guilty of terrible crimes; but if it can be proved that something in the trial was illegal, the case must be tried again. Everything about Jesus' trials was illegal, but He did not appeal for another trial.

The Servant is compared to a lamb, which is one of the frequent symbols of the Savior in Scripture. A lamb died for each Jewish household at Passover, and the Servant died for His people, the nation of Israel. Jesus is "the Lamb of God, who takes away the sin of the world!" (John 1:29); and twenty-eight times in the book of Revelation, Jesus is referred to as "the Lamb."

Since Jesus Christ was crucified with criminals as a criminal, it was logical that His dead body would be left unburied, but God had other plans. The burial of Jesus Christ is as much a part of the gospel as is His death, for the burial is proof that He actually died. The Roman authorities would not have released the body to Joseph of Arimathea and Nicodemus if the victim were not dead (see 19:38–39). A wealthy man like Joseph would never have carved out a tomb for himself so near to a place of execution, particularly when his home was miles away. He had prepared it for Jesus and had the spices and grave clothes ready for the burial (see Matt. 27:59–60). How wonderfully God fulfilled Isaiah's prophecy!

Applying God's Truth:

1. Many times Jesus' words had silenced His opponents. Why do you think He remained silent at His trial?

2. In what ways is a lamb a good symbol for Jesus? In each case, can you make the same application to *yourself?*

3. How do you feel when you are condemned for something you didn't do? What can you learn from Jesus' response in the same situation?

Day 27

The #1 Thirst Quencher

Read Isaiah 54–56

"Come, all you who are thirsty, come to the waters.... Come,
buy wine and milk without money and without cost."

ISAIAH 55:1

The invitation to come to the waters is extended to "every one" (v. 1 KJV) and not just to the Jews. Anyone who is thirsting for that which really satisfies is welcome to come. As in Isaiah 25:6, the prophet pictures God's blessings in terms of a great feast, where God is the host.

In the East, water is a precious ingredient, and an abundance of water is a special blessing. Wine, milk, and bread were staples of a Middle Eastern diet. The people of Judah were living on substitutes that did not nourish them. They needed "the real thing," which only the Lord could give. In Scripture, both water and wine are pictures of the Holy Spirit (see John 7:37–39; Eph. 5:18). Jesus is the "bread of life" (John 6:32–35), and His living Word is like milk (see 1 Peter 2:2). Our Lord probably had Isaiah 55:2 in mind when He said, "Do not work for food that spoils, but for food that endures to eternal life" (John 6:27).

People had to work hard to dig wells, care for flocks and herds, plant seed, and tend to the vineyards. But the Lord offered to them free everything they were laboring for. If they had listened to His Word, they would have been inclined to come; for God draws sinners to Himself through the Word (see 5:24). Note the emphasis on *hearing* in Isaiah 55:2–3. Jesus Christ is God's covenant to the Gentiles ("peoples," 55:4), and His promises will stand as long as His Son lives, which is forever.

Applying God's Truth:

1. What is something you have recently been "thirsting" for?

2. How does intense thirst affect your mood and productivity? How might this be true in a spiritual sense as well?

3. What are the "waters" that will eliminate your spiritual thirst? Explain.

Day 28

Truth versus Lies

Read Isaiah 57–59

"Justice is far from us, and righteousness does not reach us. We look for light, but all is darkness; for brightness, but we walk in deep shadows."

ISAIAH 59:9

There was a great deal of injustice in the land, with the rich exploiting the poor and the rulers using their authority only to make themselves rich. The people lifted their hands to worship God, but their hands were stained with blood (see 1:15, 21). God could not answer their prayers because their sins hid His face from them (see 59:2).

It was a conflict between *truth* and *lies,* just as it is today. When people live on lies, they live in a "twilight zone" and do not know where they are going. When truth falls, it creates a "traffic jam"; and justice and honesty cannot make progress. God is displeased with injustice, and He wonders that none of His people will intercede or intervene (see v. 16). So the Lord Himself intervened and brought the Babylonians to destroy Judah and Jerusalem and to teach His people that they cannot despise His law and get away with it.

God's judgment on His people was a foreshadowing of that final day of the Lord when all the nations will be judged. When it is ended, Israel will be not only God's *chosen* people but God's *cleansed* people, and the glory of the Lord will radiate from Mt. Zion.

The glory of the Lord in the promised kingdom is the theme of the closing chapters of Isaiah. While we are waiting and praying, "Thy kingdom come" (Matt. 6:10 KJV), perhaps we should also be interceding and intervening. We are the salt of the earth and the light of the world (see 5:13–14), and God expects us to make a difference.

Applying God's Truth:

1. What would you say are the primary injustices in today's society?

2. What lies still influence God's people? How do you avoid being taken in by them?

3. In what ways are you "interceding and intervening" as you await God's kingdom?

Day 29

Jubilee!

Read Isaiah 60–62

"I, the LORD, love justice; I hate robbery and iniquity. In my faithfulness I will reward them and make an everlasting covenant with them."

ISAIAH 61:8

The background of Isaiah 61 is the "Year of Jubilee" described in Leviticus 25:8ff. Every seven years, the Jews were to observe a "sabbatical year" and allow the land to rest. After seven sabbaticals, or forty-nine years, they were to celebrate the fiftieth year as the "Year of Jubilee." During that year, all debts were to be canceled, all land returned to the original owners, the slaves were to be freed, and everybody was to be given a fresh new beginning. This was the Lord's way of balancing the economy and keeping the rich from exploiting the poor.

If you have trusted Christ as your Savior, you are living today in a spiritual "Year of Jubilee." You have been set free from bondage; your spiritual debt to the Lord has been paid; you are living in "the acceptable year of the LORD" (Isa. 61:2 KJV; also quoted in Luke 4:19 KJV). Instead of the ashes of mourning, you have a crown on your head (see Isa. 61:3); for He has made you a king (see Rev. 1:6). You have been anointed with the oil of the Holy Spirit, and you wear a garment of righteousness (see Isa. 61:3).

In her days of rebellion, Israel was like a fading oak and a waterless garden (see 1:30); but in the kingdom, she will be like a watered garden (see 58:11) and a tree (oak) of righteousness (see 61:3). In their kingdom "Year of Jubilee," the Jewish people will rebuild, repair, and restore their land; and the Gentiles will shepherd Israel's flocks and herds and tend to their crops. Instead of being farmers and shepherds, the Jews will be priests and ministers! (See vv. 4–6.) God will acknowledge them as His firstborn (see Exod. 4:22) and will give them a double portion of His blessing (see Isa. 61:7).

Applying God's Truth:

1. Do you have any kind of system that ensures rest, canceled debts, and settled accounts for others on a regular basis? If not, what are some potential consequences?

2. In what ways do you demonstrate your freedom from bondage, release from spiritual debt, and so forth?

3. Can you think of a person or group you could provide with an unexpected gift of freedom and/or peace?

Day 30

Comfort King

Read Isaiah 63–66

> *"This is the one I esteem: he who is humble and
> contrite in spirit, and trembles at my word."*
>
> ISAIAH 66:2

Throughout his book, Isaiah has presented us with alternatives: Trust the Lord and live, or rebel against the Lord and die. He has explained the grace and mercy of God and offered His forgiveness. He has also explained the holiness and wrath of God and warned of His judgment. He has promised glory for those who will believe and judgment for those who scoff. He has explained the foolishness of trusting man's wisdom and the world's resources.

The prophet calls the professing people of God back to spiritual reality. He warns against hypocrisy and empty worship. He pleads for faith, obedience, a heart that delights in God, and a life that glorifies God. "'There is no peace,' says my God, 'for the wicked'" (57:21); for in order to have peace, we must have righteousness. The only way to have righteousness is through faith in Jesus Christ (see Rom. 3:19–31).

Isaiah's message has been, "Be comforted by the Lord!" *But God cannot comfort rebels!* If we are sinning against God and comfortable about it, something is radically wrong. That false comfort will lead to false confidence, and that will lead to the chastening hand of God. "Seek the LORD while he may be found" (Isa. 55:6).

"I will praise you, O LORD. Although you were angry with me, your anger has turned away and you have comforted me" (12:1).

Applying God's Truth:

1. What are some clear alternatives you are currently facing in your life?

2. In what ways do you still tend to be a rebel in God's kingdom?

3. What three things has Isaiah taught you (or reminded you of) that you feel will be most significant in your near future?

Hope

Thirty Daily Readings from the Book of 1 Peter

The eminent psychiatrist Dr. Karl Menninger called hope "the major weapon against the suicide impulse." He said that hope was "an adventure, a going forward—a confident search for a rewarding life" (*The Dictionary of Quotable Definitions*, ed. Eugene E. Brussell, Prentice-Hall).

Those of us who have trusted Christ as our Savior are not searching for hope or life, because we have both of these priceless possessions in Jesus Christ. Peter called it "a living hope"—a hope that is *alive* and that *gives us life* as we follow the Lord. A living hope makes life worth living.

All of us have days, maybe weeks, when the future looks dim, and we wonder if it is really worth it all to keep going. People, circumstances, health, finances—all of these things and more seem to conspire against us to rob us of our hope. That's when we need the "spiritual prescription" found in the ancient letter we call 1 Peter.

In this letter, the apostle explains what Christian hope is and how it changes our lives. Peter makes it clear that God's children have no reason to despair no matter how they feel or what they face in life.

So, if you have been trying to manufacture hope in your heart, and the machinery has broken down, a study of 1 Peter is just what you need. The future is always bright when you are possessed by the living hope, trusting the living Word, and guided by the living Christ.

"Like newborn babies, crave pure spiritual milk,
so that by it you may grow
up in your salvation, now that you have
tasted that the Lord is good."

1 PETER 2:2–3

Day 1

Hope: It's Alive

Read 1 Peter 5:12

*"I have written to you briefly, encouraging you and testifying
that this is the true grace of God. Stand fast in it."*

1 PETER 5:12

W hile there's life, there's hope!" That ancient Roman saying is
still quoted today, and, like most adages, it has an element of
truth but no guarantee of certainty. It is not the fact of life that determines hope, but the faith of life. A Christian believer has a "living
hope" (1:3) because his "faith and hope are in God" (v. 21). This "living hope" is the major theme of Peter's first letter. He is saying to all
believers, "Be hopeful!"

The writer's given name was Simon, but Jesus changed it to
Peter, which means "a stone" (see John 1:35–42). The Aramaic
equivalent of "Peter" is "Cephas" (v. 42), so Peter was a man with
three names. Nearly fifty times in the New Testament he is called
"Simon," and often he is called "Simon Peter." Perhaps the two
names suggest a Christian's two natures: an old nature (Simon) that
is prone to fail, and a new nature (Peter) that can give victory. As
Simon, he was only another human piece of clay, but Jesus Christ
made a rock out of him!

Applying God's Truth:

1. If Jesus changed your name (or gave you a nickname), what do you think it would be? Why?

2. Would you say that hope is alive in you? To what extent? (Thriving? A little weak? *Barely* alive? etc.)

3. What situation in your life would you say is most in need of new levels of hope?

Day 2

Three United Themes

Read 1 Peter 1:1–2

> *"Peter, an apostle of Jesus Christ, to God's elect, strangers in
> the world.... Grace and peace be yours in abundance."*
>
> 1 PETER 1:1–2

As we study 1 Peter, we will see how the three themes of suffering, grace, and glory unite to form an encouraging message for believers experiencing times of trial and persecution. These themes are summarized in 5:10, a verse we would do well to memorize.

The cynical editor and writer H. L. Mencken once defined hope as "a pathological belief in the occurrence of the impossible." But that definition does not agree with the New Testament meaning of the word. True Christian hope is more than "hope so." It is confident assurance of future glory and blessing.

This confident hope gives us the encouragement and empowerment we need for daily living. It does not put us in a rocking chair where we complacently await the return of Jesus Christ. Instead, it puts us in the marketplace, on the battlefield, where we keep on going when the burdens are heavy and the battles are hard. Hope is not a sedative; it is a shot of adrenaline, a blood transfusion. Like an anchor, our hope in Christ stabilizes us in the storms of life (see Heb. 6:18–19), but unlike an anchor, our hope moves us forward; it does not hold us back.

Applying God's Truth:

1. On a scale of 1 (least) to 10 (most), to what level do you currently feel you are experiencing suffering? God's grace? God's glory?

2. How would you explain Christian "hope" to a stranger who asked?

3. Can you think of a time in the recent past when your hope was like "a shot of adrenaline"? What were the circumstances?

Day 3

Glory Be

Read 1 Peter 1:3–5

"In his great mercy he has given us new birth into a living hope through the resurrection of Jesus Christ from the dead, and into an inheritance that can never perish, spoil or fade."

1 PETER 1:3–4

On a balmy summer day, my wife and I visited one of the world's most famous cemeteries, located at Stoke Poges, a little village not far from Windsor Castle in England. On this site Thomas Gray penned his famous "Elegy Written in a Country Churchyard," a poem most of us had to read at one time or another in school.

As we stood quietly in the midst of ancient graves, one stanza of that poem came to mind:

The boast of heraldry, the pomp of power
And all that beauty, all that wealth e're gave,
Awaits alike the inevitable hour.
The paths of glory lead but to the grave.

Man's glory simply does not last, but God's glory is eternal; and He has deigned to share that glory with us!

What do we mean by "the glory of God"? The glory of God means the sum total of all that God is and does. Glory is not a separate attribute or characteristic of God, such as His holiness, wisdom, or mercy. Everything that God is and does is characterized by glory. He is glorious in wisdom and power, so that everything He thinks and does is marked by glory. He reveals His glory in creation (see Ps. 19:1–6), in His dealings with the people of Israel, and especially in His plan of salvation for lost sinners.

Applying God's Truth:

1. Prior to this reading, what would have been your definition of God's "glory"?

2. How have you recently witnessed God's glory expressed in creation?

3. How have you recently witnessed God's glory in other ways in your life?

Day 4

Why Trials?

Read 1 Peter 1:6–7

> *"In this you greatly rejoice, though now for a little while you may have had to suffer grief in all kinds of trials."*
>
> 1 PETER 1:6

All God plans and performs here is preparation for what He has in store for us in heaven. He is preparing us for the life and service yet to come. Nobody yet knows all that is in store for us in heaven, but this we do know: Life today is a school in which God trains us for our future ministry in eternity. This explains the presence of trials in our lives—they are some of God's tools and textbooks in the school of Christian experience.

Peter illustrated this truth by referring to the goldsmith (see v. 7). No goldsmith would deliberately waste the precious ore. He would put it into the smelting furnace long enough to remove the cheap impurities; then he would pour it out and make from it a beautiful article of value. It has been said that the Eastern goldsmith kept the metal in the furnace until he could see his face reflected in it. So our Lord keeps us in the furnace of suffering until we reflect the glory and beauty of Jesus Christ.

Applying God's Truth:

1. What have some of your previous trials taught you about God that you might not have known otherwise?

2. What have your previous trials taught you about yourself?

3. As you dwell on many of the trials that you have overcome with God's grace, what are some things you can be sure of as you face present trials?

Day 5

If We Could See It, It Wouldn't Be Faith

Read 1 Peter 1:8–12

"Even though you do not see him now, you believe in him and are filled with an inexpressible and glorious joy, for you are receiving the goal of your faith, the salvation of your souls."

1 PETER 1:8–9

We must live by faith and not by sight (see 2 Cor. 5:7). An elderly lady fell and broke her leg while attending a summer Bible conference. She said to the pastor who visited her, "I know the Lord led me to the conference. But I don't see why this had to happen! And I don't see any good coming from it." Wisely, the pastor replied, "Romans 8:28 doesn't say we *see* all things working together for good. It says that we *know* it."

Faith means surrendering all to God and obeying His Word in spite of circumstances and consequences. Love and faith go together: When we love someone, we trust that person. And faith and love together help to strengthen hope; for where we find faith and love, we will find confidence for the future.

How can we grow in faith during times of testing and suffering? The same way we grow in faith when things seem to be going well: by feeding on the Word of God (see Rom. 10:17). Our fellowship with Christ through God's Word not only strengthens our faith, it also deepens our love. It is a basic principle of Christian living that we spend much time in the Word when God is testing us and Satan is tempting us.

Applying God's Truth:

1. Even though you can't see God, would you say your faith is "blind"? Explain.

2. What is an issue of faith you are really struggling with at this time because you can't "see" an answer? As you struggle, what is your goal?

3. When you are facing difficult times, do you have favorite passages of Scripture you go to? (Ask this question to three other people this week and "trade" favorite verses to expand your collection.)

Day 6

Mind Control

Read 1 Peter 1:13–16

"Prepare your minds for action; be self-controlled; set your hope fully on the grace to be given you when Jesus Christ is revealed."

1 PETER 1:13

"Prepare your minds for action" (or, "Gird up the loins of your mind" [KJV]) simply means, "Pull your thoughts together! Have a disciplined mind!" The image is that of a robed man, tucking his skirts under his belt, so he can be free to run. When we center our thoughts on the return of Christ, and live accordingly, we escape the many worldly things that would encumber our mind and hinder our spiritual progress.

Outlook determines outcome; attitude determines action. A Christian who is looking for the glory of God has a greater motivation for present obedience than a Christian who is ignoring the Lord's return.

Not only should we have a disciplined mind, but we should have a sober and optimistic mind as well. The result of having a spiritual mind-set is that we experience the grace of God in our life. To be sure, we will experience grace when we see Jesus Christ, but we can also experience grace today as we look for Him to return. We have been saved by grace (see Eph. 2:8–9), and we depend moment by moment on God's grace. Looking for Christ to return strengthens our faith and hope in difficult days, which imparts to us more of the grace of God.

Applying God's Truth:

1. In what ways do you "prepare your mind for action" in a spiritual sense?

2. Do you feel that you are "self-controlled" when it comes to your thoughts and attitudes? In what areas do you need improvement?

3. To what extent do you feel that you "experience the grace of God in your life"? What might you do to increase your awareness of His grace?

Day 7

The Privilege Not Granted

Read 1 Peter 1:17

> *"Since you call on a Father who judges each man's work impartially,*
> *live your lives as strangers here in reverent fear."*
>
> 1 PETER 1:17

God will give us many gifts and privileges as we grow in the Christian life, but He will never give us the privilege to disobey and sin. He never pampers His children or indulges them. He is not a respecter of persons (see Acts 10:34 KJV). He "shows no partiality and accepts no bribes" (Deut. 10:17). "For God does not show favoritism" (Rom. 2:11). Years of obedience cannot purchase an hour of disobedience. If one of His children disobeys, God must chasten (see Heb. 12:1–13). But when His child obeys and serves Him in love, He notes that obedience and service and prepares the proper reward.

Peter reminds us that we are only sojourners on earth. Life is too short to waste in disobedience and sin (see 1 Peter 4:1–6). It was when Lot stopped being a sojourner, and became a resident in Sodom, that he lost his consecration and his testimony (see Gen. 13). Everything he lived for went up in smoke! (See chaps. 18–19.) We must keep reminding ourselves that we are "strangers and pilgrims" in this world.

In view of the fact that the Father lovingly disciplines His children today, and will judge their works in the future, we ought to cultivate an attitude of "godly fear" (Heb. 12:28 KJV). This is not the cringing fear of a slave before a master, but the loving reverence of a child before his father. It is not fear of His judgment, but a fear of disappointing Him or sinning against His love. It is a sober reverence for the Father.

Applying God's Truth:

1. Have you given up sins that you occasionally wish you could indulge in again—perhaps just for a few minutes?

2. Do you think it is fair that Christians are expected to obey God's law all the time while the rest of the world "lives it up" as they please? Explain.

3. What would you say is the difference between fear and "godly fear"?

Day 8

Leaving Slavery Behind

Read 1 Peter 1:18–21

> *"You know that it was not with perishable things such as silver and gold that you were redeemed ... but with the precious blood of Christ."*
>
> 1 PETER 1:18–19

The love of God is the highest motive for holy living. Peter reminded his readers of their salvation experience, a reminder that all of us regularly need to hear. He reminded them of what they were. They were slaves who needed to be set free.

There were probably fifty million slaves in the Roman Empire! Many slaves became Christians and fellowshipped in the local assemblies. Slaves could purchase their own freedom, if they could collect sufficient funds; or their masters could sell them to someone who would pay the price and set them free. Redemption was a precious thing in that day.

We must never forget the slavery of sin. Not only did we have a life of slavery, but it was also a life of emptiness. At the time, we may have thought our lives were full and happy, when they were really empty and miserable. In the same way, unsaved people today are blindly living on substitutes.

While ministering in Canada, I met a woman who told me she had been converted early in life but had drifted into a "society life" that was exciting and satisfied her ego. One day, she was driving to a card party and happened to tune in a Christian radio broadcast. At that very moment, the speaker said, "Some of you women know more about cards than you do your Bible!" Those words arrested her. God spoke to her heart, she went back home, and from that hour her life was dedicated fully to God. She saw the futility and vanity of a life spent out of the will of God.

Applying God's Truth:

1. What types of "slavery" did you experience prior to becoming a Christian?

2. Does "holy living" ever seem like "boring living" to you? If so, how do you generate more excitement about living as God has instructed?

3. What are some "substitutes" that people try (rather than a personal relationship with God) as they seek to fill the emptiness in their lives?

Day 9

Milk: It Does a Body Good

Read 1 Peter 1:22–2:3

"Like newborn babies, crave pure spiritual milk, so that by it you may grow up in your salvation, now that you have tasted that the Lord is good."

1 PETER 2:2–3

God's Word *has* life, *gives* life, and *nourishes* life. We should have appetites for the Word just like hungry newborn babes! We should want the pure Word, unadulterated, because it alone can help us grow. When I was a child, I did not like to drink milk (and my father worked for the Borden Dairy!), so my mother used to add various syrups and powders to make my milk tastier. None of them really ever worked. It is sad when we Christians have no appetite for God's Word, but must be "fed" religious entertainment instead. As we grow, we discover that the Word is milk for babes, but also strong meat for the mature (see Heb. 5:11–14; 1 Cor. 3:1–4). It is also bread (see Matt. 4:4) and honey (see Ps. 119:103).

Sometimes children have no appetite because they have been eating the wrong things. Peter warns us to lay aside certain wrong attitudes of heart that would hinder our appetite and spiritual growth. When we are growing in the Word, we are peacemakers, not troublemakers, and we promote the unity of the church.

Applying God's Truth:

1. If you received physical nourishment with the same regularity that you receive spiritual nourishment from God's Word, what kind of shape would you be in?

2. In what way(s) does God's Word *give* you life? How does it *nourish* your life?

3. Can you think of anything you have been "nibbling on" lately that might affect your spiritual appetite?

Day 10

All Together Now!

Read 1 Peter 2:4–8

"As you come to him, the living Stone—rejected by men but chosen by God and precious to him—you also, like living stones, are being built into a spiritual house."

1 PETER 2:4–5

Peter wrote this letter to believers living in five different provinces, yet he said that they all belonged to one "spiritual house." There is a unity of God's people that transcends all local and individual assemblies and fellowships. We belong to each other because we belong to Christ.

A contractor in Michigan was building a house, and the construction of the first floor went smoothly. But when the workers started on the second floor, they had nothing but trouble. None of the materials from the lumberyard would fit properly. Then they discovered the reason: They were working with two different sets of blueprints! Once they got rid of the old set, everything went well, and they built a lovely house.

Too often, we Christians hinder the building of the church because we are following the wrong plans. When Solomon built his temple, his workmen followed the plans so carefully that everything fit together on the construction site (see 1 Kings 6:7). If all of us would follow God's blueprints, given in His Word, we would be able to work together without discord and build His church for His glory.

Applying God's Truth:

1. On a scale of 1 (least) to 10 (most), how much unity would you say your immediate family has? Your church? Your workplace?

2. Can you think of a time when you tried to "build" according to your own blueprints rather than God's? What happened?

3. Think of three people you have frequent conflicts with (or whom you try to avoid). What might you do to try to create better unity with each person?

Day 11

Family, Stones, Priests, Citizens

Read 1 Peter 2:9–10

> *"You are a chosen people, a royal priesthood, a holy nation, a people belonging to God, that you may declare the praises of him who called you out of darkness into his wonderful light."*
>
> 1 PETER 2:9

We belong to one family of God and share the same divine nature. We are living stones in one building and priests serving in one temple. We are citizens of the same heavenly homeland. It is Jesus Christ who is the source and center of this unity. If we center our attention and affection on Him, we will walk and work together; if we focus on ourselves, we will only cause division.

Unity does not eliminate diversity. Not all children in a family are alike, nor are all the stones in a building identical. In fact, it is diversity that gives beauty and richness to a family or building. The absence of diversity is not *unity;* it is *uniformity*, and uniformity is dull. It is fine when the choir sings in unison, but it is preferable that they sing in harmony.

Christians can differ and still get along. All who cherish the "one faith" and who seek to honor the "one Lord" can love one other and walk together (see Eph. 4:1–6). God may call us into different ministries, or to use different methods, but we can still love each other and seek to present a united witness to the world.

St. Augustine said it perfectly: "In essentials, unity. In nonessentials, liberty. In all things, charity."

Applying God's Truth:

1. Which of Peter's analogies (family, stones, priests, citizens) do you think best describes God's people? Why?

2. What are some examples where people try to substitute uniformity for unity, and only end up making things worse?

3. Can you think of a personal example where diversity of individuals combined for the unity of a group and resulted in the glory of God?

Day 12

People Are Watching

Read 1 Peter 2:11–12

"Live such good lives among the pagans that, though they accuse you of doing wrong, they may see your good deeds and glorify God on the day he visits us."

1 PETER 2:12

In the summer of 1805, a number of Indian chiefs and warriors met in council at Buffalo Creek, New York, to hear a presentation of the Christian message by a Mr. Cram from the Boston Missionary Society. After the sermon, a response was given by Red Jacket, one of the leading chiefs. Among other things, the chief said:

"Brother, you say there is but one way to worship and serve the Great Spirit. If there is but one religion, why do you white people differ so much about it? Why not all agree, as you can all read the Book?

"Brother, we are told that you have been preaching to the white people in this place. These people are our neighbors. We are acquainted with them. We will wait a little while and see what effect your preaching has upon them. If we find it does them good, makes them honest and less disposed to cheat Indians, we will then consider again of what you have said."

Peter encourages us to bear witness to the lost, by word and deed, so that one day God might visit them and save them. When these people do trust Christ, they will glorify God and give thanks because we were faithful to witness to them even when they made life difficult for us.

Applying God's Truth:

1. Can you recall a time when you were trying to follow another person's example, only to be disappointed when that individual let you down in some way? How might you avoid such disappointments in the future?

2. Who are the people who look at you as an example for what a Christian should be?

3. Are you satisfied with the example you set for others? If not, how can you improve it?

Day 13

Politically Correct

Read 1 Peter 2:13–25

*"Show proper respect to everyone: Love the brotherhood
of believers, fear God, honor the king."*

1 PETER 2:17

True Christians submit to authority because they are first of all submitted to Christ. They use their freedom as a tool to build with and not as a weapon to fight with. A good example of this attitude is Nehemiah, who willingly gave up his own rights that he might help his people and restore the walls of Jerusalem (see Neh. 1:1–7:3).

If we are sincerely submitted to authority "for the Lord's sake" (see 1 Peter 2:13), then we will show honor to all who deserve it. We may not agree with their politics or their practices, but we must respect their position (see Rom. 13:1–6). We will also "love the brotherhood," meaning, of course, the people of God in the church. This is a recurring theme in this letter. One way we show love to the brotherhood is by submitting to the authority of the "powers that be" (v. 1 KJV) for we are bound together with one another in our Christian witness.

We "honor the king" because we "fear God." It is worth noting that the tenses of these verbs indicate that we should *constantly* maintain these attitudes. "Keep loving the brotherhood! Keep fearing God! Keep honoring the king!"

Applying God's Truth:

1. Do you know Christians who frequently criticize national or local politicians? Do *you* do so? Do you think such criticism has anything to do with submitting to their authority? Explain.

2. When *you* are in a position of authority, what do you do to try to earn the respect of those under your control?

3. On a scale of 1 (least) to 10 (most), where would you stand on loving the brotherhood? Fearing God? Honoring political leaders?

Day 14

Commotion versus Commitment

Read 1 Peter 3:1–2

> *"Wives, in the same way be submissive to your husbands so that,*
> *if any of them do not believe the word, they may be won over*
> *without words by the behavior of their wives."*

1 PETER 3:1

While standing in the checkout line in a supermarket, I over-heard two women discussing the latest Hollywood scandal that was featured on the front page of a tabloid displayed on the counter. As I listened (and I could not *help* but hear them!), I thought: "How foolish to worry about the sinful lives of matinee idols. Why clutter up your mind with such trash? Why not get acquainted with decent people and learn from their lives?"

When Christian couples try to imitate the world and get their standards from Hollywood instead of from heaven, there will be trouble in the home. But if both partners will imitate Jesus Christ in His submission and obedience, and His desire to serve others, then there will be triumph and joy in the home.

A psychiatrist friend of mine states that the best thing a Christian husband can do is pattern himself after Jesus Christ. In Christ we see a beautiful blending of strength and tenderness, and that is what it takes to be a successful husband.

We cannot follow Christ's example unless we first know Him as our Savior, and then submit to Him as our Lord. We must spend time with Him each day, meditating on the Word and praying, and a

Christian husband and wife must pray together and seek to encourage each other in the faith.

Applying God's Truth:

1. How many celebrity marriages or breakups can you recall from the "news" during the past several months? Why do you think so many people find such things newsworthy?

2. What couple do you know who best demonstrates the meaning of real love? What do you think is their "secret"?

3. In order of priority, what are the top ten characteristics you admire (or desire) in your spouse (or potential spouse)?

Day 15

Submission and Attraction

Read 1 Peter 3:3–6

"Your beauty ... should be that of your inner self, the unfading beauty
of a gentle and quiet spirit, which is of great worth in God's sight."

1 PETER 3:3–4

It is the character and conduct of the wife that will win the lost husband—not arguments, but such attitudes as submission,
understanding, love, kindness, patience. These qualities are not man-
ufactured; they are the fruit of the Spirit (see Gal. 5:22–23) that
comes when couples are submitted to Christ and to one another.

One of the greatest examples of a godly wife and mother in
church history is Monica, the mother of the famous St. Augustine.
God used Monica's witness and prayers to win both her son and her
husband to Christ, though her husband was not converted until
shortly before his death. Augustine wrote in his *Confessions*, "She
served him as her lord, and did her diligence to win him unto Thee
... preaching Thee unto him by her conversation [behavior]; by
which Thou ornamentest her, making her reverently amiable unto
her husband."

In a Christian home, couples must minister to one other. A
Christian husband must minister to his wife and help to beautify her
in the Lord (see Eph. 5:25–30). A Christian wife must encourage her
husband and help him grow strong in the Lord. If there are unsaved
people in the home, they will be won to Christ more by what they see
in lives and relationships than by what they hear in witness.

Applying God's Truth:

1. What letter grade would you give yourself in each of the following "subjects": Submission? Understanding? Love? Kindness? Patience?

2. Can you think of a specific instance when you chose to be submissive and accomplished much more good than if you had argued your case?

3. If an unsaved person had witnessed your actions this past week, do you think that individual would want to become a Christian? Why?

Day 16

Ignorance Is Amiss

"Husbands, in the same way be considerate as you live with your wives, and treat them with respect as the weaker partner and as heirs with you of the gracious gift of life, so that nothing will hinder your prayers."

1 PETER 3:7

Somebody asked Mrs. Albert Einstein if she understood Dr. Einstein's theory of relativity, and she replied, "No, but I understand the Doctor." In my premarital counseling as a pastor, I often gave the couple pads of paper and asked them to write down the three things each one thought the other enjoyed doing the most. Usually, the prospective bride made her list immediately; the groom would sit and ponder. And usually the woman was right but the man wrong! What a beginning for a marriage!

It is amazing that two people can make plans to live together the rest of their lives and not really know each other! Ignorance is dangerous in any area of life, but it is especially dangerous in marriage. A Christian husband needs to know his wife's moods, feelings, needs, fears, and hopes. He needs to "listen with the heart" and share meaningful communication with her. There must be in the home such a protective atmosphere of love and submission that the husband and wife can disagree and still be happy together. When either mate is afraid to be open and honest about a matter, then the couple is building walls and not bridges.

Applying God's Truth:

1. What are three things you might like to do on your next free night? (If married, see how many of these things your spouse predicts you will say.)

2. If neither of you is very good at "listening with the heart," what are some things you and your spouse might try to improve your listening skills?

3. What are three things you can do to be able to disagree with your spouse and still be happy together?

Day 17

Response Options

Read 1 Peter 3:8–12

"Do not repay evil with evil or insult with insult, but with blessing, because to this you were called so that you may inherit a blessing."

1 PETER 3:9

As Christians, we can live on one of three levels. We can return evil for good, which is the satanic level. We can return good for good and evil for evil, which is the human level. Or, we can return good for evil, which is the divine level. Jesus is the perfect example of this latter approach (see 2:21–23). As God's loving children, we must not give "eye for eye, and tooth for tooth" (see Matt. 5:38–48), which is the basis for *justice*. We must operate on the basis of mercy, for that is the way God deals with us.

We must always be reminded of our *calling* as Christians, for this will help us love our enemies and do them good when they treat us badly (see Luke 6:27). We are called to "inherit a blessing." The persecutions we experience on earth today only add to our blessed inheritance of glory in heaven someday (see Matt. 5:10–12). But we also inherit a blessing *today* when we treat our enemies with love and mercy. By sharing a blessing with them, we receive a blessing ourselves! Persecution can be a time of spiritual enrichment for believers. The saints and martyrs in church history all bear witness to this fact.

Applying God's Truth:

1. Can you think of a relationship you have with someone that continues to be bad because neither of you will make the first move toward reconciliation? What would it take for you to be willing to make the first move this week?

2. When was the last time you returned good for evil? Why do you think it is such an infrequent option for most people?

3. How much of an effort do you make to genuinely love your enemies? What are some new things you might try?

Day 18

Fearless (or, at Least, Less Fear)

Read 1 Peter 3:13–17

"Who is going to harm you if you are eager to do good? But even if you should suffer for what is right, you are blessed."

1 PETER 3:13–14

As Christians, we are faced with crises, and we are tempted to give in to our fears and make the wrong decisions. But if we "set apart Christ as Lord" (v. 15) in our hearts, we need never fear people or circumstances. Our enemies may hurt us, but they can never harm us. Only we can harm ourselves if we fail to trust God. Generally speaking, people do not oppose us if we do good; but even if they do, it is better to suffer for righteousness' sake than to compromise our testimony.

Instead of experiencing fear as we face the enemy, we can experience blessing, if Jesus Christ is Lord in our hearts. When Jesus Christ is Lord of our lives, each crisis becomes an opportunity for witness. We should "always be prepared to give an answer" (v. 15). As Christians we should be able to give a reasoned defense of our hope in Christ, *especially in hopeless situations*. A crisis creates the opportunity for witness when we behave with faith and hope, because nonbelievers will then sit up and take notice.

Applying God's Truth:

1. Do you ever experience elements of fear in any part of your spiritual life?

2. What is the worst you have ever suffered because of your faith?

3. Under what situations are you most tempted to compromise your faith? Or are you consistently firm when dealing with bosses, strangers, skeptics, and others?

Day 19

Act Now

Read 1 Peter 3:18–20

"[Christ] went and preached to the spirits in prison who disobeyed long ago when God waited patiently in the days of Noah while the ark was being built."
1 PETER 3:19–20

Jesus Christ is the only Savior, and the lost world needs to hear His gospel. Some people try to use this complex passage of Scripture to prove a "second chance for salvation after death." But even if these "spirits" were those of unsaved people, this passage says nothing about their salvation. And why would Jesus offer salvation (if He did) *only to sinners from Noah's day?* And why did Peter use a different verb meaning "proclaim as a herald" instead of the usual word for "preach the gospel"?

Hebrews 9:27 makes it clear that death ends the opportunity for salvation. This is why the church needs to get concerned about evangelism and missions, because people are dying who have never even heard the good news of salvation, let alone had the opportunity to reject it. It does us no good to quibble about differing interpretations of a difficult passage of Scripture if what we *do* believe does not motivate us to share the gospel with others.

Peter made it clear that difficult days give us multiplied opportunities for witness.

Are we taking advantage of our opportunities?

Applying God's Truth:

1. How might this difficult passage be used in a discussion of "Is there life after death"?

2. When you consider that "death ends the opportunity for salvation," can you think of anyone with whom you want or need to spend more time in order to share some spiritual truths?

3. Have you set any spiritual goals that you hope to accomplish before your own death?

Day 20

Noah Way

Read 1 Peter 3:20–22

"In it [the ark] only a few people, eight in all, were saved through water,
and this water symbolizes baptism that now saves you also."

1 PETER 3:20–21

W hat relationship did Peter see between his readers and the ministry of Noah? For one thing, Noah was a "preacher of righteousness" (2 Peter 2:5) during a very difficult time in history. The early Christians knew that Jesus had promised that, before His return, the world would become like the "days of Noah" (Matt. 24:37–39); and they were expecting Him soon (see 2 Peter 3:1–13). As they saw society decay around them and persecution begin, they would think of the Lord's words.

Noah was a man of faith who kept doing the will of God even when he seemed to be a failure. This would certainly be an encouragement to Peter's readers. If we measured faithfulness by results, then Noah would get a very low grade. Yet God ranked him very high!

But this is another connection: Peter saw in the Flood a picture (type) of a Christian's experience of baptism. The Flood pictures death, burial, and resurrection. The waters buried the earth in judgment, but they also lifted Noah and his family up to safety. The early church saw in the ark a picture of salvation. Noah and his family were saved by faith because they believed God and entered into the ark of safety. So sinners are saved by faith when they trust Christ and become one with Him.

Applying God's Truth:

1. What sinful things have you witnessed this week that would have made Noah feel right at home?

2. What aspects of being a Christian might seem as absurd to outsiders as Noah's building an ark? How do you handle skepticism others may have toward your faith?

3. If Noah were to offer you advice about being a godly example in a sinful world, what do you think he might tell you?

Day 21

Used to the Dark?

Read 1 Peter 4:1–3

"Since Christ suffered in his body, arm yourselves also with the same attitude, because he who has suffered in his body is done with sin."

1 PETER 4:1

The picture in verse 1 is that of a soldier who puts on equipment and arms in preparation for battle. Our attitudes are weapons, and weak or wrong attitudes will lead us to defeat. Outlook determines outcome, and we must have the right attitudes if we are to live a right life.

A friend and I met at a restaurant to have lunch. It was one of those places where the lights are low, and people need a miner's helmet to find their table. We had been seated several minutes before we started looking at the menu, and I remarked that I was amazed how easily I could read it. "Yes," said my friend, "it doesn't take us long to get accustomed to the darkness."

There is a sermon in that sentence: It is easy for us Christians to get accustomed to sin. Instead of having a militant attitude that hates and opposes it, we gradually get used to sin, sometimes without even realizing it. The one thing that will destroy "the rest of [our] earthly life" (v. 2) is sin. A believer living in sin is a terrible weapon in the hands of Satan.

Applying God's Truth:

1. In what ways have your attitudes of the past week been "weapons"?

2. What are some sins that many Christians gradually get used to?

3. Can you identify any "dim" areas in your own life where the light of God's truth needs to shine through more brightly?

Day 22

Lost Patience

Read 1 Peter 4:4–6

> *"[The pagans] think it strange that you do not plunge with them into the same flood of dissipation, and they heap abuse on you."*
>
> 1 PETER 4:4

Unsaved people do not understand the radical change that their friends experience when they trust Christ and become children of God. They do not think it strange when people wreck their bodies, destroy their homes, and ruin their lives by running from one sin to another! But let a drunkard become sober, or an immoral person pure, and they think that individual has gone crazy!

We must be patient toward the lost, even though we do not agree with their lifestyles or participate in their sins. After all, unsaved people are blind to spiritual truth (see 2 Cor. 4:3–4) and dead to spiritual enjoyment (see Eph. 2:1). In fact, our contact with the lost is important to them since we are the bearers of the truth that they need. When the unsaved attack us, it is our opportunity to witness to them (see 1 Peter 3:15).

The unsaved may judge us, but one day God will judge them. Instead of arguing with them, we should pray for them, knowing that the final judgment is with God.

Applying God's Truth:

1. Do you know an unsaved person who is a real annoyance, yet for whom you may be the sole contact with Christianity? What can you do to maintain that relationship?

2. When you are annoyed or antagonized by lost people, what steps can you take to remain patient?

3. You may feel you are making no progress with your unsaved associates, but do you think the situation might change the next time they go through an intense emotional crisis? In what ways?

Day 23

Time Matters

Read 1 Peter 4:7–11

> *"The end of all things is near. Therefore be clear minded
> and self-controlled so that you can pray."*
>
> 1 PETER 4:7

My wife and I were in Nairobi, Kenya, where I would be minis-tering to several hundred national pastors at an Africa Inland Mission conference. We were very excited about the conference even though we were a bit weary from the long air journey. We could hardly wait to get started, and the leader of the conference detected our impatience.

"You are in Africa now," he said to me in a fatherly fashion, "and the first thing you want to do is put away your watch."

In the days that followed, as we ministered in Kenya and Zaire, we learned the wisdom of his words. Unfortunately, when we returned to the States, we found ourselves caught up again in the clockwork prison of deadlines and schedules.

Peter had a great deal to say about *time*. Certainly the awareness of his own impending martyrdom had something to do with this emphasis (see John 21:15–19; 2 Peter 1:12ff). If we really believe in eternity, then we will make the best use of time. If we are convinced that Jesus is coming, then we will want to live prepared lives. Whether Jesus comes first, or death comes first, we want to make "the rest of [our] time" (1 Peter 4:2 KJV) count for eternity. And we can!

Applying God's Truth:

1. In what ways do you tend to get too caught up "in the clockwork prison of deadlines and schedules"?

2. In what ways do you tend to squander time, and not get around to what you feel is important?

3. What do you need to do to achieve the right balance—to do what you want to do without becoming a slave to the clock?

Day 24

The Privilege of Suffering

Read 1 Peter 4:12–16

"Rejoice that you participate in the sufferings of Christ,
so that you may be overjoyed when his glory is revealed."

1 PETER 4:13

It is an honor and a privilege to suffer with Christ and be treated by the world the way it treated Him. "The fellowship of sharing in his sufferings" is a gift from God (see Phil. 1:29; 3:10). Not all believers grow to the point where God can trust them with this kind of experience, so we ought to rejoice when the privilege comes to us (see Acts 5:41).

Christ is with us in the furnace of persecution. When the three Hebrew children were cast into the fiery furnace, they discovered they were not alone (see Dan. 3:23–25). The Lord was with Paul in all of his trials, and He promises to be with us "to the very end of the age" (Matt. 28:20). In fact, when sinners persecute us, they are really persecuting Jesus Christ (see Acts 9:1–4).

"Suffering" and "glory" are twin truths that are woven into the fabric of Peter's letter. The world believes that the *absence* of suffering means glory, but as Christians our outlook is different. The trial of our faith today is the assurance of glory when Jesus returns (see 1 Peter 1:7–8). This was the experience of our Lord (see 5:1), and it will also be our experience.

Applying God's Truth:

1. Does suffering ever feel like a privilege to you? If not, how can you try to keep a positive mind-set as you suffer?

2. How do you think suffering is connected with glory?

3. Do you think you can ever suffer anything that Jesus doesn't completely understand? Explain.

Day 25

Acts of Faith

Read 1 Peter 4:17–19

"Those who suffer according to God's will should commit themselves
to their faithful Creator and continue to do good."

1 PETER 4:19

If we really have hope, and believe that Jesus is coming again, then we will obey His Word and start laying up treasures and glory in heaven (see Matt. 6:19–20 KJV). Unsaved people have a present that is controlled by the past, but Christians have a present that is controlled by the future (see Phil. 3:12–21). In our very serving, we are committing ourselves to God and making investments for the future.

There is a striking illustration of this truth in Jeremiah 32. The prophet Jeremiah had been telling the people that one day their situation would change, and they would be restored to their land. But at that time, the Babylonian army occupied the land and was about to take Jerusalem. Jeremiah's cousin, Hanamel, gave Jeremiah an option to purchase the family land *that was occupied at the time by enemy soldiers.* The prophet had to "put his money where his mouth was." And he did it! As an act of faith, he purchased the land and became, no doubt, the laughingstock of the people of Jerusalem. But God honored his faith because Jeremiah lived according to the Word that he preached.

Applying God's Truth:

1. In what ways is your present controlled by your past? How is it controlled by your future?

2. Can you think of an act of faith you have performed along the lines of Jeremiah's buying a field—something that made absolutely no sense to the rest of the world, yet that showed your complete trust in God?

3. Rather than focusing on obstacles, what things can you list that should tend to help you "commit [yourself] to [your] faithful Creator and continue to do good"?

Day 26

Forward Ho!

Read 1 Peter 5:1–3

"Be shepherds of God's flock that is under your care, serving as overseers—not because you must, but because you are willing, as God wants you to be."

1 PETER 5:2

Pastors of local assemblies must be a people who walk with God and who are growing in their spiritual life. Paul admonished young Timothy: "Be diligent in these matters; give yourself wholly to them, so that everyone may see your progress" (1 Tim. 4:15). The word "progress" in the original means "pioneer advance." Elders must constantly be moving into new territories of study, achievement, and ministry. If the leaders of the church are not moving forward, the church will not move forward.

"We love our pastor," a fine church member said to me during a conference, "but we get tired of the same thing all the time. He repeats himself and doesn't seem to know that there are other books in the Bible besides Psalms and Revelation." That pastor needed to become a "spiritual pioneer" and move into new territory, so that he might lead his people into new blessings and challenges.

Sometimes God permits trials to come to a church so that the people will be forced to grow and discover new truths and new opportunities. Certainly Peter grew in his spiritual experience as he suffered for Christ in the city of Jerusalem. He was not perfect by any means, but Peter was yielded to Christ and willing to learn all that God had for him.

Applying God's Truth:

1. On a scale of 1 (least) to 10 (most), how would you rate your pastor in terms of being a "spiritual pioneer"? How would you evaluate your own recent "advances"?

2. What have you done lately to encourage your pastor and/or church officers?

3. Can you think of an example of how trials have helped your church grow spiritually? What can you learn from those past trials?

Day 27

Reward Offered

"When the Chief Shepherd appears, you will receive the crown of glory that will never fade away."

1 PETER 5:4

Christian workers may labor for many different kinds of rewards. Some work hard to build personal empires; others strive for the applause of men; still others seek promotion in their denomination. All of these things will "fade away" one day. The only reward we ought to strive for is the "Well done!" of the Savior (see Matt. 25:21–23) and the unfading "crown of glory" that goes with it. What a joy it will be to place the crown at His feet (see Rev. 4:10) and acknowledge that all we did was because of His grace and power (see 1 Cor. 15:10; 1 Peter 4:11). We will have no desire for personal glory when we see Jesus Christ face-to-face.

Everything in the local church rises or falls with leadership. No matter how large or small a fellowship may be, the leaders must be Christians, each with a vital personal relationship with Jesus, a loving concern for people, and a real desire to please God.

We lead by serving, and we serve by suffering. This is the way Jesus did it, and this is the only way that truly glorifies Him.

Applying God's Truth:

1. Be honest. What kinds of rewards do you hope to receive *now* for your Christian service? What *eventual* rewards do you desire?

2. In what ways do you lead by serving? How do you serve by suffering?

3. What would you tell someone who is complaining that it is unfair to have a life of suffering *now* in order to receive rewards *later?*

Day 28

A Fashion Statement

Read 1 Peter 5:5–7

> *"Clothe yourselves with humility toward one another, because,*
> *'God opposes the proud but gives grace to the humble.'"*
>
> 1 PETER 5:5

Younger believers should submit to the older believers, not only out of respect for their age, but also out of respect for their spiritual maturity. Not every "senior saint" is a mature Christian, of course, because quantity of years is no guarantee of quality of experience. This is not to suggest that the older church members should "run the church" and never listen to the younger members! Too often there is a generation war in the church, with the older people resisting change, and the younger people resisting the older people!

The solution is twofold: (1) all believers, young and old, should submit to one other; and (2) all should submit to God. "Clothe yourselves with humility" is the answer to the problem. Just as Jesus laid aside His outer garments and put on a towel to become a servant (see John 13:1–17), so each of us should have a servant's attitude and minister to one other. True humility is described in Philippians 2:1–11. Humility is not demeaning ourselves and thinking poorly of ourselves. It is simply not thinking of ourselves at all!

Applying God's Truth:

1. Would you say you are usually submissive to older Christians? Are there exceptions? Explain.

2. How would potential problems with submitting to other people be avoided if everyone regularly submitted to God?

3. Would you say you "clothe [yourself] with humility"? In what ways? How could you improve in this area?

Day 29

Take It from Peter

Read 1 Peter 5:8–11

"Be self-controlled and alert. Your enemy the devil prowls around like a roaring lion looking for someone to devour."

1 PETER 5:8

We should never discuss things with Satan or his associates. Eve made this mistake, and we all know the sad consequences (see Gen. 3:1–24). Also, we should never try to fight Satan in our own way. We should resist him the way Jesus did, with the Word of God (see Luke 4:1–13). We must never get the idea that we are the only ones going through battles, because Peter has told us "your brothers throughout the world" are facing the same trials (1 Peter 5:9). We must pray for one another and encourage each other in the Lord. And we must remember that our personal victories will help others, just as their victories will help us.

Had Peter obeyed these instructions the night Jesus was arrested, he would not have gone to sleep in the Garden of Gethsemane (see Matt. 26:36–46), attacked Malchus (see John 18:10), or denied the Lord (see Matt. 26:69–75). He did not take the Lord's warning seriously; in fact, he argued with Him! (See vv. 31–35.) Nor did he recognize Satan when the adversary inflated his ego with pride, told him he did not have to "watch and pray," and then incited him to use his sword. Had Peter listened to the Lord and resisted the enemy, he would have escaped all those failures.

Before we can stand before Satan, we must bow before God. Peter resisted the Lord and ended up submitting to Satan!

Applying God's Truth:

1. What do you suppose was Peter's biggest regret from his life?

2. When Christians feel they are alone in their spiritual struggles, how is Satan's influence more effective? How can this problem be alleviated?

3. It is easy to see how Peter could have avoided some of his failures, but can you look back on your own life and see what you could have done differently to avoid some major failures?

Day 30

A Peace at a Time

Read 1 Peter 5:12–14

"Greet one another with a kiss of love. Peace to all of you who are in Christ."

1 PETER 5:14

Paul always ended his letters with a benediction of grace (see 2 Thess. 3:17–18). Peter closed this epistle with a benediction of peace. He opened the letter with a greeting of peace (1 Peter 1:1–2), so the entire epistle points to God's peace from beginning to end. What a wonderful way to end a letter that announced the coming of a "fiery trial" (4:12 KJV)!

Four times in the New Testament we find the admonition about "a holy kiss" (see Rom. 16:16; 1 Cor. 16:20; 2 Cor. 13:12; and 1 Thess. 5:26). Peter called it "a kiss of love." Keep in mind that the men kissed the men, and the women kissed the women. It was a standard form of greeting or farewell in that part of the world at that time, just as it is in many Latin countries today. How wonderful that Christian slaves and masters would so greet each other "in Christ"!

Peter has given to us a precious letter that encourages us to hope in the Lord no matter how trying the times may be. Down through the centuries, the church has experienced various "fiery trials," and yet Satan has not been able to destroy it. The church today is facing a "fiery trial," and we must be prepared.

But, whatever may come, Peter is still saying to each of us—be hopeful! The glory is soon to come!

Applying God's Truth:

1. Do you think it is unusual that a message about "fiery trials" would have such an emphasis on peace? Explain.

2. Do you have a greeting that is equivalent to "a kiss of love"? If not, can you think of one you might want to initiate?

3. Are you any more hopeful now than when you started reading 1 Peter? If so, in what ways?